TULSA CITY-COUNTY LIBRARY

MAY - ' 2023

WHAT IS DEMOCRACY?

We the People:
U.S. Government at Work

Kevin Winn

Published in the United States of America by:

CHERRY LAKE PRESS
2395 South Huron Parkway, Suite 200, Ann Arbor, Michigan 48104
www.cherrylakepress.com

Reading Adviser: Beth Walker Gambro, MS, Ed., Reading Consultant, Yorkville, IL
Content Adviser: Mark Richards, Ph.D., Professor, Dept. of Political Science, Grand Valley State University, Allendale, MI

Photo Credits: cover: © Prostock-studio/Shutterstock; page 5: © SeventyFour/Shutterstock; page 6: © Sumit Saraswat/Shutterstock; page 7: © Loredana Sangiuliano/Shutterstock; page 8: © W. Scott McGill/Shutterstock; page 9: © CiEll/Shutterstock (top), U.S. Census Bureau (bottom); page 11: © Stephanie Frey/Shutterstock; page 12: © Cory Woodruff/Shutterstock; page 13: Document Bank of Virginia; page 14: Library of Congress, Records of the National Women's Party; page 16: © Sharkshock/Shutterstock; page 19: © lev radin/Shutterstock; page 20: © nimito/Shutterstock; page 21 © Joseph Sohm/Shutterstock

Copyright © 2023 by Cherry Lake Publishing Group

All rights reserved. No part of this book may be reproduced or utilized in any form or by any means without written permission from the publisher.

Cherry Lake Press is an imprint of Cherry Lake Publishing Group.

Library of Congress Cataloging-in-Publication Data

Names: Winn, Kevin P., author.
Title: What is democracy? / Kevin Winn.
Description: Ann Arbor, Michigan : Cherry Lake Publishing, [2023] | Series: We the people: U.S. government at work | Audience: Grades 2-3
Summary: "Young readers will discover what exactly democracy is and learn about the basic building blocks of the United States of America. They'll also learn how they play a key role in American democracy. Series is aligned to 21st Century Skills curriculum standards. Engaging inquiry-based sidebars encourage students to Think, Create, Guess, and Ask Questions. Includes table of contents, glossary, index, author biography, and sidebars"— Provided by publisher.
Identifiers: LCCN 2022039928 | ISBN 9781668920398 (paperback) | ISBN 9781668919378 (hardcover) | ISBN 9781668923054 (pdf) | ISBN 9781668921722 (ebook)
Subjects: LCSH: Democracy—United States—Juvenile literature. | United States—Politics and government—Juvenile literature.
Classification: LCC JK1025 .W56 2023 | DDC 328.73–dc23/eng/20221007
LC record available at https://lccn.loc.gov/2022039928

Cherry Lake Press would like to acknowledge the work of the Partnership for 21st Century Learning, a Network of Battelle for Kids. Please visit http://www.battelleforkids.org/networks/p21 for more information.

Printed in the United States of America
Corporate Graphics

CONTENTS

Chapter 1: What Is Democracy?   4

Chapter 2: Democracy's History in the United States   10

Chapter 3: The Current State of Democracy   17

Activity	20
Glossary	22
Find Out More	23
Index	24
About the Author	24

WHAT IS DEMOCRACY?

Democracy is a necessary part of the way the United States **governs**, or rules, itself. It gives people the power to affect the government and laws. In a democracy, people choose their leaders. But what does democracy mean?

A democracy is a type of government. It means that people choose the way they're governed. Many countries have some sort of democracy.

Citizens in a democracy vote for leaders.

Some may have a **parliament**. Others might use a **constitution**. The United States has a **representative democracy**. This means we elect people to represent us in our government. A part of this system makes sure that people living in states with fewer people have a voice in how they are governed.

Citizens of democracies around the world vote for leaders.

Many countries have some form of democratic government. Make a list of five different countries with a democracy. What are the differences between them? What are the similarities? Look to see if the countries you chose have a constitution, a prime minister, or a president.

Through the U.S. Constitution, the founders of the United States made sure each state had representation in the government. They did this by creating two different houses in Congress. They are the Senate and the House of Representatives.

The Senate has two senators from each state. There are 100 members. The House of Representatives has 435 members. Each state has at least one representative.

Create!

Look up your senators and representatives. Choose one. Send a letter or email to them explaining something you think they should fix. Include why this is an important issue to you.

States with more people have more representatives. For example, California has 52 Representatives. Vermont and Delaware each only have one.

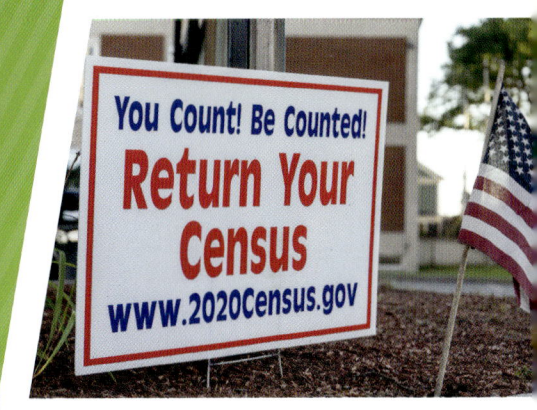

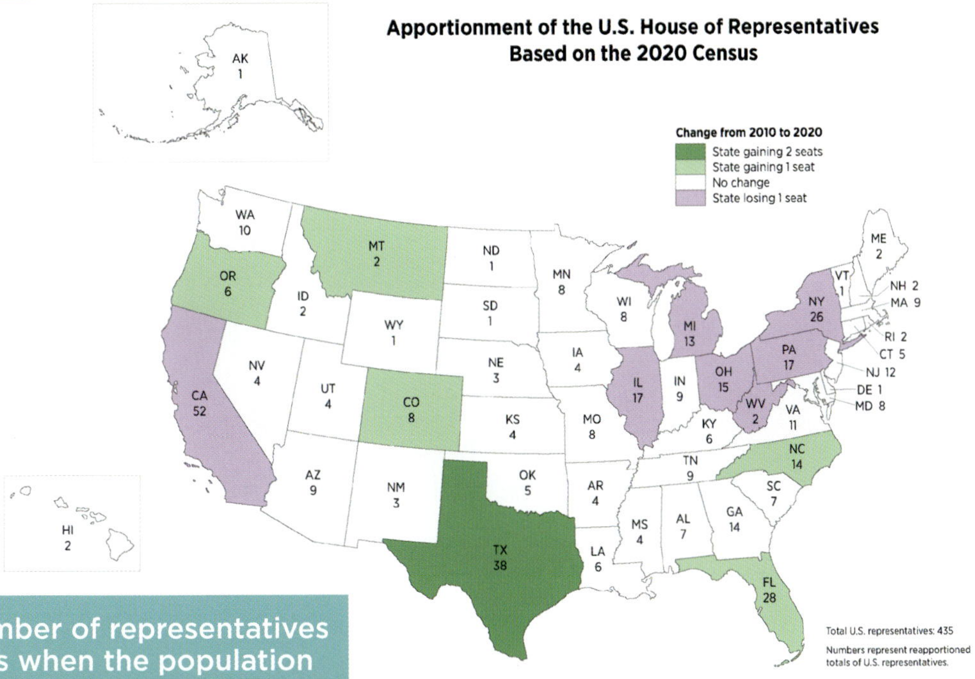

Apportionment of the U.S. House of Representatives Based on the 2020 Census

Change from 2010 to 2020
- State gaining 2 seats
- State gaining 1 seat
- No change
- State losing 1 seat

AK 1
WA 10
MT 2
ND 1
MN 8
ME 2
VT 1
NH 2
MA 9
OR 6
ID 2
SD 1
WI 8
MI 13
NY 26
RI 2
CT 5
NJ 12
DE 1
MD 8
NV 4
WY 1
NE 3
IA 4
IL 17
IN 9
OH 15
PA 17
CA 52
UT 4
CO 8
KS 4
MO 8
KY 6
WV 2
VA 11
AZ 9
NM 3
OK 5
AR 4
TN 9
NC 14
SC 7
HI 2
TX 38
LA 6
MS 4
AL 7
GA 14
FL 28

Total U.S. representatives: 435
Numbers represent reapportioned totals of U.S. representatives.

The number of representatives changes when the population changes.

9

DEMOCRACY'S HISTORY IN THE UNITED STATES

The U.S. form of democracy plays a role in the world. It has inspired other countries to adopt democracies. It has spread useful ideas to the rest of the world. This includes having a constitution that gives its citizens certain rights.

Democracy hasn't always been a sure thing in the United States. Not all people have been

11

The first 10 amendments are also called the Bill of Rights.

represented throughout U.S. history. Originally, only White men could vote. This history of **inequity** inspired people to fight for their rights. This led to changes to the U.S. Constitution. These changes are called amendments.

Activists have worked hard to make sure more people's voices are a part of the government.

Their efforts have helped our democracy. It led to new amendments to the Constitution. These gave rights to more people. The Fifteenth Amendment gave men of color the right to vote. The Nineteenth Amendment expanded voting rights to women.

Women organized and protested to have their right to vote protected in the Constitution.

Thousands of amendments to the U.S. Constitution have been proposed. But only 27 have been passed. Adding an amendment to the Constitution is a complex process. Many people need to support the amendment. This is why activists are important.

Think!

The Constitution plays an important role in our country, but it isn't perfect. That's why it has amendments. Choose one amendment. Why do you think it's important? Why was it added?

Long lines can leave people waiting hours to vote.

THE CURRENT STATE OF DEMOCRACY

Trust is an important part of democracy. When we vote for a person to represent us, we trust they were elected fairly. We also trust this person will keep the promises they make as they **campaign**.

Democracy is **fragile**. It relies on the goodwill of the people. Sometimes our democracy's strength is tested. One example happened on January 6, 2021.

A group of people who didn't trust our democracy attacked the U.S. Capitol. This event made many Americans think. They realized we should not take democracy for granted.

Protests are important. They are a constitutional right. But violence and destruction of property is not.

Democracy is important to our way of life. It helps the United States move forward. Together, we can help make it stronger. This includes protecting everyone's right to participate in our government.

Ask Questions!

Sometimes people are unable to participate in our democracy. This happens when lawmakers make it difficult for people to vote. For example, people without access to cars or buses may not be able to get to a polling place. What are ways we can address this? Discuss your thoughts with a friend and family member. What do they think?

Protests are important. They are a constitutional right. But violence and destruction of property is not.

ACTIVITY

Let your voice be heard! Voting in elections is important. Research how many polling places your state has. Research where your nearest polling place is. Choose another state. How many polling places does it have? Are there more or fewer than your state? What did you find surprising?